Confidence

The Science & Art of Self-Belief

Steve Knox

Title: Confidence: The Science & Art of Self-Belief
Author: Knox, Steve
ISBNs: 978-0-6481300-0-0 (paperback)
         978-0-6481300-1-7 (epub)

Special Sales: This title is available in special quantity discounts. Custom printing or excerpting can also be done to fit specific needs. For more information please visit steveknox.us

THANK YOU

Meghan — This book wouldn't be possible without your help and encouragement.

Joan, Debbie and Phil — For the privilege of your wisdom and counsel.

Family and friends — Especially the 'Table of Knowledge': Johnny, Billy, Mark, Adam, Paul and Michael.

My clients — You know who you are and what this conversation means.

You — Thank you for reading this book. I wrote it for you (and me).

A WORD BEFORE

My story as the son of an engineer and an artist, combined with over a decade of research from coaching and consulting, has led me to the hypothesis that anyone can develop confidence.

It's not an elusive leadership trait, it can be learned.

By you.

Confidence: The Science & Art of Self-Belief is divided into two parts: the first defines confidence, and the second is a daily reading for developing confidence.

The goal of the book is simple: help you move from self-doubt to self-belief. Every single person has struggled somewhere along the way with trusting themself.

This is a simple guide for developing the confidence you need to overcome whatever challenge you're facing.

The second part of the book is designed to be read slowly. It's a meditative guide based on the ancient practice of Lectio Divina. ThrityOne daily readings to help you build confidence.

Before you open the daily reading, take ten deep breaths. Read it through once, then re-read it contemplatively.

And if you're really courageous, invite a friend to read it with you.

I hope this book educates and inspires you.

CONTENTS

Part I: The Science & Art of Self-Belief
- Confidence in the Flesh
- What is Confidence?

Part II: Lectio Divina

Part III: ThirtyOne Days to Confidence

Daily Readings

Day 1 - Worry

Day 2 – Insecurity

Day 3 – Fear

Day 4 – Hopelessness

Day 5 – Apathy

Day 6 – Avoidance

Day 7 – Comfort

Day 8 – People-Pleasing

Day 9 – Conflict

Day 10 – Boredom

Day 11 – Isolation

Day 12 – Regret

Day 13 – Overthinking

Day 14 – Chaos

Day 15 – Laziness

Day 16 – Faith

Day 17 – Help

Day 18 – Progress

Day 19 – Perfection

Day 20 – Must

Day 21 – Self-Care

Day 22 – Risk

Day 23 – Consistency

Day 24 – Openness

Day 25 – Honesty

Day 26 – Willingness

Day 27 – Kindness

Day 28 – Humility

Day 29 – Generosity

Day 30 – Confidence

Day 31 – Courage

Part IV: Definitions and Cited Sources

Part V: About the Author, Steve Knox

THE SCIENCE & ART OF SELF-BELIEF

Confidence early 15c., from Middle French and Latin confidentia *'firmly trusting, bold,'* present participle of confidere 'to have full trust or reliance,' from assimilated form of com, here probably an intensive prefix (see com-), + fidere 'to trust.'

'Because one believes in oneself, one doesn't try to convince others. Because one is content with oneself, one doesn't need others' approval. Because one accepts oneself, the whole world accepts him or her.'

— Lao Tzu

'If you hear a voice within you say you cannot paint, then by all means paint and that voice will be silenced.'

— Vincent van Gogh

'Once we believe in ourselves, we can risk curiosity, wonder, spontaneous delight, or any experience that reveals the human spirit.'

— E. E. Cummings

'Everyone thinks of changing the world, but no one thinks of changing himself.'

— Leo Tolstoy

Quotes on the left-hand side of each daily reading can be attributed to *The Asymmetrical Leader: Embrace Your Weaknesses, Unleash Your Strengths.*

CONFIDENCE IN THE FLESH

I watched a blind man leap off a cliff.

It was a sunny Thursday afternoon in Rio De Janeiro, Brazil. I was accompanying a group of college students from Houston, Texas to help with community service projects in the favelas of Niteroi.

This was our first day of R&R on the trip and we decided to see the beautiful sites of the city. Our host and translator suggested we visit one of the highest parks in Rio overlooking the bay in-between the two Brazilian sister cities of Rio and Niteroi.

When we arrived at the top it was stunning, we could see everything — the cities stretching into the distance, the bright and dark shades of the green tropical landscape, the edge of the coastline snaking beside the azure blue ocean.

We noticed a group of parachuters gathered around an edge of the park's many cliffs. In turns they, either in tandem or individually, prepared their parachutes, waited for the perfect gust of wind then jumped off the cliff and flew gracefully down to the beach far below.

The wind was a major factor in the safety of a takeoff. If it suddenly changed, it could cause tangled parachutes, personal injuries or even death.

A tandem group stepped up to the launch point. They were strapped in together. Their parachute went up, caught a bit of air, the wind changed and slammed them and the parachute into the pavement.

They got up, stepped onto the ledge a little shakier, and prepared to jump again. The wind lifted the parachute, pulling them to their toes, they were going to jump — but once more, the wind shifted and they were thrown backwards into the pavement.

I remember thinking, "Something is wrong, these two guys are different, what's going on?"

I asked our translator and she informed me the two jumpers were friends and one was blind. A good mate agreed to his blind friend's wish of taking him parachuting so he could feel the thrill and freedom of flying.

What a friendship. What trust. What inspiration.

We all wanted their jump to be successful.

With help, the two picked themselves up from the pavement for a third attempt. Talk about hutzpah. Talk about grit. Talk about confidence.

They got into position, the wind caught their parachute and it lifted them high above our group and they flew. We cheered.

We witnessed something awesome. And, collectively watched in amazement as the two glided slowly, beautifully, down to the beach below.

Real Confidence

Watching these two courageous souls taught me that confidence is never a solo adventure.

It takes real confidence to strap your blind friend to you and jump off the side of a mountain.

It takes that same confidence to be blind and trust your friend enough to jump too.

That's what confidence does — it moves you to take healthy risks for the sake of those you love so that they and you can experience more of life — so you can truly and fully live.

WHAT IS CONFIDENCE?

Textbook Definitions

Confidence is hard to define, but easy to recognise. It literally means, '*to trust within.*'

Trust is another word for faith. Faith is belief.

So in a real sense, confidence is believing in yourself. Here's a simple equation that illustrates confidence ...

$$Challenge + Competence = Confidence.$$

Challenges reveal what you're made of and what you're lacking. Competence is all about your abilities, knowledge, skills and experience.

My leading question when sitting down with a potential client is always, 'What are your biggest challenges?'

I lead with this because 9 times out of 10, the heart of the issue is a lack of self-belief. It's not about having the right plan of attack (which is important).

It's never about how talented and educated you might be (which definitely helps).

The key to overcoming any challenge you face in life always lies in your ability to trust yourself.

To believe you are competent enough to overcome any challenge facing you.

To be confident.

The two questions you should ask yourself when faced with a challenge:

1. Have I faced a situation like this before?
2. Do I have the knowledge, skills and experience to overcome it?

If you answer *no* to the first question, go find a friend, mentor or coach who can help you.

If you answer no to the second question, go to work on yourself. Take a class, read 10 books on the subject, research it and then come back to face it head on.

And if and when you fail, use that experience as feedback.

Edison famously believed he never failed, he only found 10,000 ways that didn't work. Churchill believed success was stumbling from one failure to the next with enthusiasm. And, Ford believed failure was just an opportunity to intelligently begin again.

Talk about redefining failure.

Failure does not define you. It refines you.

What is your attitude about facing the challenges in your life?

Does fear overtake you? Does it freeze you in your tracks? Does it cause you to overthink? Or perhaps try to escape?

How many times have you been at your physical or emotional breaking point and either made a bad decision, hurt someone else or yourself in the process?

Why?

Because you were living reactively.

Afraid.

Fear

When a challenge is greater than your ability, fear is the natural result.

For thousands of years humans have been hardwired with a fight or flight response. When in danger your nervous system goes into overdrive.

It's how you survive.

This is great when there's a potential predator after you, but not helpful if you are trying to function and progress in normal society.

Fear of the unknown (or the known) is the opposite of faith. When you give in to the 'what-ifs' and your insecurities, you rob yourself of personal growth and the chance to improve.

Everyone experiences fear. That's just normal life happening.

The best remedy for fear is curiosity.

The next time fear kicks in, don't run. Instead, explore your emotions. Question your thoughts. Pay attention to the cause and effect of what created the situation.

Again, faith is the opposite of fear. So trust the facts of who you are and what you have to offer.

Boredom

When you're not challenged boredom is the natural result. You can guarantee it.

If you're constantly bored, chances are it's been a long time since you put yourself in a place where you were forced to learn or grow.

All growth happens at the edge of your comfort zone — just beyond where you feel safe and sound.

If you're deeply honest you've settled. You've grown complacent.

Don't lose heart. Embrace that frustration. Look into it. It's a window into what really motivates you.

When you're bored you have a clear choice:

Stay and slowly become a lesser version of yourself.

Or, shake things up by trying new things and improving yourself.

When you're in a job or a relationship that feels stagnant you will quickly lose interest. As a human, you are hardwired for growth and progress.

You crave development — personally and professionally. That's why dead ends are called dead ends.

If you stay too long numbness turns into apathy.

Apathy

Apathy is literally a lack of passion. It's when you just don't care about anything. Work becomes a boring routine. Relationships become a chore.

You simply check out — mentally and emotionally.

Being apathetic is a serious risk. Medically, it's a sign of depression. While I'm not a doctor, I have seen this over and over in clients.

If you're apathetic you stopped caring somewhere along the way. Maybe it was in response to past trauma. Maybe it was in response to extreme disappointment. Or maybe, you stopped believing your future was worth fighting for.

I've been there.

I let apathy grip my heart. I went to a dark place for quite a while. I went through a season of life where I stopped caring because I felt trapped. I isolated myself.

The bad news is that it's impossible to grow outside of community. You can't do it. This life is about relationships. Apathy is a subconscious cry for help. It's a defence mechanism and a SOS signal to everyone in your life.

I've been there.

I had to reinvent myself to break out of my fixed mindset. Some caring, kind and generous people helped me back to my feet.

Humility comes through humiliations. It's difficult to admit you need other people. But, you do. You really do. If you're struggling with apathy, you can break free.

You can change your mindset.

You can change the story you're telling yourself.

And, you can change. But, you have to reach out, you have to act.

Your Brain and Confidence

Over the past decade heaps of research has been focused on the neuroplasticity of the human brain. Plasticity means malleable.

Your brain can change. Even in old age.

In his book, *The Brain That Changes Itself*, psychologist and researcher Norman Doidge explains that your brain is a living organ that can actually change its own structure and function, throughout your life and even into old age.

That's pretty awesome news.

So if you feel or think you are stuck, you simply need to change your thinking — and change your thinking — again, and again and again.

Be mindful of what situations and stresses cause you to feel less than.

Be brave and explore the emotions linked to the thoughts that make you feel worthless. Identify what triggers cause these negative thoughts and make a plan to change them. You've got to practice over and over being honest and choosing a positive mindset.

When you change your thoughts, you create new neural pathways in your brain and repetition strengthens them so eventually they become the 'normal' pathway your brain will choose when dealing with a specific situation or decision.

You've got be patient with yourself.

Changing negative thoughts and behaviours takes time.

Research at University of College London, confirms that it takes a minimum of two months to change your brain's chemistry.

The Orbitofrontal Cortex

In 2016, *Time Magazine* reported on a new confidence study published in the journal *Neuron*.

Researchers at Cold Spring Harbor Laboratory performed a study with rats which helped them learn more about the brain and the origins of confidence.

The study confirmed that rats will wait longer for a reward after they successfully completed a test. Researchers taught the rats the right ways to complete the test; the pathways that produced a reward. When the rats chose correctly, they patiently waited on their reward because they were confident in their choices.

From these outcomes, scientists were able to measure the time rats were willing to wait and use this information to create a model to predict the likelihood of correct decisions based on wait time and an objective measure to track the rats' feelings of confidence.

While participating in this study, scientists noticed the rats' Orbitfrontal Cortex, the OFC, was an area of the brain involved in the rats' decision making and wait times. It was hypothesised the OFC, if inactivated, would cause the rats to lose their ability to successfully complete the tests.

Surprisingly, when the OFC was inactivated, the rats were still able to make correct choices and move through the tests successfully. But, the time they waited for a reward (even if they completed the test successfully) changed. The rats were not as patient and did not wait for a reward because they did not know if they were correct, they lacked confidence in their performance and choices. Wait time could no longer predict if they had successfully completed the course.

Humans are not like rats, we are definitively more complex and intelligent. However, this study does highlight a couple of important insights.

You can learn the skill of confidence.

By practicing it, you can cultivate it, you can grow it, you can strengthen it.

You can come to depend on it.

And you can make strong and wise choices even if you do not have a feeling to confirm it.

You will make mistakes. Learn from them, explore what you learn.

It's okay if you do not 'feel' confident, like the rats when their OFC was inactivated. Look at your past successes, mistakes, lessons learned. Trust these experiences and use them to guide you.

And most importantly trust yourself — be confident.

Decision-Making

Confidence plays a major role in decision-making.

The more confident you are, the better you are at trusting yourself in the heat of the moment.

Past experience strengthens self-belief. When you trust yourself, you make better decisions.

Recent research has proven your brain, 'produces feelings of confidence that inform decisions the same way statistics pull patterns out of noisy data'.

When you feel confident, you make objective calculations. It sounds counterintuitive, but your intuition has logical underpinnings.

If you've lost confidence, you have probably made a string of bad decisions repeatedly which have created a negative pattern of thinking in your brain. A mental rut.

This type of fearful thinking leads to a fixed or static mindset. You begin to see everything through a negative lens.

While being pessimistic and deliberative can bring positive insights, if this mindset becomes a pattern of behaviour you will undoubtedly move towards apathy.

The best way to adopt a different mindset is to think back on a past successful experience. Break down what happened ...

What was your approach to success?

Who were you with?

Why did you succeed?

How can you repeat this success?

By returning to a past success and thoughtfully considering it, you can create a roadmap for building confidence in facing future challenges.

In psychology this is called modelling. When you use this type of self-reflection you are building stronger neural pathways and connections in your brain.

In short, you are building confidence.

The Way Forward

Confidence is a skill that can be developed.

I've seen it happen over and over in different clients I've coached, and in my own journey as well.

It takes time, awareness, practice, and a bit of failure to build self-belief. You cannot rush this process.

In the next section of the book, I've written ThirtyOne meditations to help you cultivate confidence. Read one each day. They are quick reads, taking only two minutes to read, but I would encourage you to slow down, think about each section, and start your day mindfully.

Use this book as a journal.

It's designed to help you rediscover how much you have to offer the world.

It all starts with trusting yourself — being confident in who you are and in the gifts with which you've been entrusted.

LECTIO DIVINA

This is my modern day take on the 13th century ancient Benedictine practice of Lectio Divina, 'divine reading', for building confidence.

There are different ways to meditate. I am using a contemplative method in this book as a simple daily reading and process for reflection — a thought to help you build confidence one day at a time.

Each reading is around two minutes, but I recommend slowing down to gain the full benefits of this simple daily habit.

Lectio Divina, is a Latin term meaning 'divine reading' which describes an ancient meditative way of reading a holy text to inform your everyday life.

In the 12th century, a Carthusian monk named Guigo, described the stages he believed were essential to the practice of Lectio Divina.

The first stage is lectio (reading) where you read the passage slowly, methodically and reflectively so that it sinks into you.

The second stage is meditatio (reflection) where you think about the text and meditate upon it and how it applies to your everyday life.

The third stage is oratio (response) where you leave your thinking aside and meditatively respond to the meaning you find in the passage.

The final stage of Lectio Divina is contemplatio (rest) where you let go of trying to control your life. You simply rest in the present moment. You listen at the deepest level of your being. As you listen, you are gradually transformed from within.

These stages of Lectio Divina are not fixed rules of procedure but simple guidelines for how to build this life-changing practice.

Take these ThirtyOne days to read, think, meditate, and live in the present moment.

worry

/'wərē/

Stop doubting and start living in the truth that there are no accidental people in the universe. Every single soul exists for a reason. Everyone you lock eyes with is of immense value. This includes YOU.

Day One — Worry

READ

Worry means to 'grab by the throat and rip'. That's what worry does … it rips the life out of you. Worry feeds off future fear or past regret. Both rob you of the ability to be present. Here. Now. When you worry you feel better. It's a mind trick. A neurological trap.

When you worry your mind feels like it is doing something productive. It's not. The opposite of worry is peaceful focus — mindfulness.

THINK

How is worry robbing me of the ability to be present?

MEDITATE

Today has enough trouble and opportunity of its own. I choose to not let future worry or past guilt weigh me down and distract me. Today I consciously choose to live. Despite the burden of yesterday and my fear of tomorrow, I will be here now.

LIVE

When worry tries to choke me I will take a deep breath and return to the present.

insecurity

/ˌinsəˈkyo͝orədē/

Fulfilment in life comes when you discover and live out your unique calling, when you put your soul into your relationships, your work, your life.

Day Two — Insecurity

READ

Insecurity is a sure sign of a lack of self-belief. The ego must inflate or deflate as a result. If you're insecure you're not comfortable in your own skin. You're not okay. In a real sense you're unsure of who you are, what you have to offer and how you can add value. This is what insecurity does — it immediately kicks your brain into fight or flight mode. Your mind scans the environment noticing every potential threat.

Comparison, self-pity and false pride kick in as a mental security blanket. All of which are self-defeating forms of a scarcity mindset — your mind focusing on what you don't have. Change your mindset by embracing your insecurity. What you're lacking is an opportunity to improve, learn and grow.

THINK

Where do my biggest insecurities lie?

MEDITATE

Today I will embrace my insecurity. I will be honest about how I feel without letting my thoughts defeat me. I won't shrink back. Today I will choose to be okay with what I'm missing, what I'm lacking and where I fall short. Today I will be comfortable in my own skin.

LIVE

When insecurity kicks in I will pay attention to my thoughts and explore them as an opportunity for growth.

fear

/ˈfir/

When you do not use a gift you've been given,
eventually you lose that gift. When you do not invest
your time and talents, they waste away.

Day Three — Fear

READ
Fear is crippling. It comes from the Greek word 'phobos' or 'phobia' as it is commonly referred to today. In the Latin it means, 'to run, or flee.' Fear is how people have survived throughout human existence: See threat. Avoid or kill threat. Survive. There are hundreds of phobias — some researchers estimate 530 in total. Psychologists define fear as, 'a vital response to physical and emotional danger'. Fear is a gift. It humbles you and reminds you of your humanity. The deep-seated emotion you experience educates you about how confident you are. You cannot fake it. Curiosity is the best way to navigate and understand the fear you're facing.

THINK
How is my fear actually a powerful tool I can use for good?

MEDITATE
Today I will embrace my fears. I will not let them cripple me. Today I will feel the full weight of them and be reminded that I am alive. Today I will realise that I am not my fearful thoughts. I am simply experiencing them. I am not at their mercy. I will explore the good and the bad that comes my way.

LIVE
When fear arises in me today, I will humbly move towards it with curiosity.

hopelessness

/ˈhōpləsnəs/

You have the power to change your life by changing your story. This requires courage, discipline and perspective.

Day Four — Hopelessness

READ

Without hope people die. Even the smallest glimmer of a better future will keep you alive in the valleys of life. Hope is like water. You cannot go more than a few days without it. Learned hopelessness is a sure sign of a sick soul. Usually this type of scarcity mindset erodes your confidence daily. When you lack hope you feel like you cannot move: change, grow or improve. You feel trapped. Stuck. Isolated. Forgotten. What you cannot change you endure. With that endurance comes a bit of confidence — a small seed of hope.

THINK

When was the last time I truly felt hopeful?

MEDITATE

Today I will search for even the smallest glimmer of change, growth and progress. I will hold on to it. Nurture and cultivate it. When the dark thoughts of fear, insecurity and worry rear their ugly heads, I will remember and celebrate the good in my life. Today I will be hopeful.

LIVE

When hopelessness grips my heart, I will acknowledge it and focus on the good in my life no matter how small it may seem.

apathy

/ˈapəTHē/

Say yes. Yes to commitment. Yes to effort.
Yes to possibility. Yes to hard work. Yes to passion.
Yes to progress. Yes to your future.

Day Five — Apathy

READ

Apathy is a heart gone dark. It's the number one indicator that you are lacking a challenge worthy of your best self. Apathy weakens and isolates you. In the Latin it literally means 'a lack of passion for life'. Without passion you have nothing to fight for. Nothing to contribute. Nothing to wake up to. Without a challenge your strengths, talents, and innate gifts atrophy. Apathy is the antithesis of compassion — to suffer with others. Apathy is a negative state of being. The best way to shake it off and work through it is to take action. Apathy cannot survive serving others.

When you serve others you gain perspective. You become grateful. You change.

THINK

Where have I stopped caring about myself and others?

MEDITATE

Today I will not live a 'status quo' life. I refuse to conduct today with an apathetic approach. Today I will find a challenge worthy of my best self. I will move towards it with faith in my natural abilities. Trusting myself and even the smallest good that I can do in the world today.

LIVE

Wherever apathy is taking root in my life, I will kill it by serving others — offering a kind word, a helping hand or even a smile today.

avoidance

/əˈvoidəns/

Do not be afraid of pain. Pain is part of life. Trying to avoid pain is like trying to avoid living. Embrace it. Feel it. Be stronger from it.

Day Six — Avoidance

READ

The avoidance of pain or discomfort easily becomes a pattern for living. It sounds counterintuitive, but the only way to experience freedom is to endure hardship. To embrace some form of suffering, pain or cost. There are no shortcuts to building confidence and genuine fulfilment. It is the fight that makes the journey meaningful. Staying the course builds self-belief — confidence. It is through failure wisdom is gained. Struggle not only marks you, it makes you — stronger. There is no such thing as a 'good life' without experiencing the 'bad' as well.

THINK

Where am I avoiding pain and discomfort?

MEDITATE

Today I will continue to head towards hard and difficult situations. I will follow through and fight the temptation to turn tail and run. Today I will stand and stay. I will fight for what matters most. Today I will embrace hardship so that I can truly live the good life.

LIVE

Whenever feelings of avoidance creep up in me today, I will patiently endure.

comfort

/ˈkəmfərt/

When you get tired, keep going. When you hit the wall, keep working. Stick to your plan. Stay faithful.

Day Seven — Comfort

READ

Comfort in and of itself is not a bad thing. It comes from the 17th century French word, 'to strengthen'. A life of comfort sounds ideal, but if you're always taking, always seeking affirmation, constantly looking for the easy way out you can be assured you will not grow. Real strength comes from testing yourself on the edge of what's comfortable, known — familiar. If you're never tested how can you know what you're capable of? Leaving the safe place for the unknown always reveals and strengthens your character. It is the ancient 'hero's journey' that every noble person seeking to live a meaningful life embraces. Creature comforts are traps. Overconsumption always leads to a dulling of the senses. When you develop an inner reservoir of strength you will seek to comfort others rather than be comforted.

THINK

Where am I seeking external comforts rather than relying on inner strength?

MEDITATE

Today I will take a conscious step beyond the edge of what I know and am comfortable with. Today I will risk in a healthy way. I will search inside myself rather than outside myself for affirmation and the approval of others. Today I will live with a conviction to challenge myself.

LIVE

Rather than sit back, I will take a healthy calculated risk.

people-pleasing

/ˈpēpəl ˈplēziNG/

So many people have stated this truth in so many ways: a sure way to fail is to try and please everyone. The only way to be fulfilled is to be faithful. Full of faith. Trusting that you are enough. That you are okay.

Day Eight — People-Pleasing

READ
The fear of rejection is real. Being on the outside looking in is never fun. Missing out and not belonging almost always leads to resentment, judgement and people- pleasing. Constantly seeking to fit in or be accepted is a clear indicator that you are lacking confidence. Every person on the planet has been rejected at some point.

Deep down everyone wants to be liked and accepted. Belonging is a basic psychological need. It's healthy. But, if you are always trying to make other people happy you will guarantee you own unhappiness. People-pleasing will erode your self-belief. Self-acceptance is the foundation for building self-belief. Loneliness, heartache and rejection are just normal life happening. Take it in stride. Don't beat yourself up or react out of fear. Have faith. You matter. You belong.

THINK
How has people-pleasing eroded my self-belief?

MEDITATE
Today I will seek to live less for the approval of others and more from a place of self-respect and humility. I will accept the fact I am accepted. Just like I am. I will be grateful for the relationships and friendships I do have. Today I will live according to my own sense of fulfilment and core values. Today I choose me.

LIVE
When rejection comes my way, I will remember that I belong.

conflict

/ˈkänˌflikt/

Believe in yourself when others doubt you.
Believe in yourself when others abandon you.
Believe in yourself
when others take advantage of you.

Day Nine — Conflict

READ

When it comes to building confidence there is no neutral ground. None. In the Latin, conflict literally means, 'to strike against'. Initially you may think that the battle is external. It's not. Conflict is internal. Self-doubt and self-rejection are always near. All you can do is all you can do. Don't overthink things. Don't beat yourself up. On one side is a challenge that scares the hell out of you and demands your very best. On the other side is apathy. Doing nothing robs you of everything. What do you have to lose? Take a risk. If your best is not enough, congratulations, you have an opportunity to learn and improve. This may mean unlearning or relearning or starting from scratch. All of which are uncomfortable. Hard. Difficult. And, trying. Life happens on the edge. Fight for your future, not with yourself.

THINK

How has internal conflict stunted my growth?

MEDITATE

Today I choose to not beat myself up. Today I will not overthink things. Instead I will choose to head out to the edge of what I know. I will move towards difficult and challenging situations for the sake of personal growth. I will face my inner demons of self-doubt and self-rejection and grow stronger. Today I will fight.

LIVE

Today I will risk and live fully.

boredom

/ˈbôrdəm/

Refuse to place blame, make excuses or get distracted. Rather, take ownership of your life, be accountable for your choices, and feel the full responsibility and weight to leave your unique mark on the world.

Day Ten — Boredom

READ

Boredom is a lack of imagination. It's the absence of mental stimulation — a challenge that captures your best thinking. Constant boredom is a clear sign that you are overqualified or over-skilled for the work you're doing. You're uninspired. The opposite of boredom is attention — your mind engaged, alive, creative.

Boredom erodes confidence, because you're missing the opportunity to develop new skills and sharpen old ones. A lack of action leads to mental atrophy. Your best thinking requires a challenge worthy of your best self. When restlessness kicks in, harness it and use that space to explore a new opportunity or a different perspective. Get curious. Don't give in to sluggishness or laziness. Choose to take a breath, enjoy the downtime and observe your thoughts.

THINK

Where has boredom made me lazy?

MEDITATE

Today I will see an opportunity in boredom. I will explore my boredom and the time it affords me. Today I will pivot away from laziness towards intentionality. Today I will take advantage of 'downtime' and be curious about what is happening in and around me. Today I will pay attention.

LIVE

When boredom comes my way, I will use it for self-reflection.

isolation

/ˌīsəˈlāSH(ə)n/

If you want to be successful in designing a life of impact you cannot go it alone. You must have someone you trust who can give you feedback and encouragement when you fall down, lose track or mess up.

Day Eleven — Isolation

READ

Isolation is hell on earth. It's impossible to grow outside the context of community. Confident people can be alone in a crowd without being lonely. Loneliness is a normal part of the human experience, but isolation is something different altogether. Being known is scary. Solitary confinement is scarier. Totally cutting yourself off from people only hinders your personal growth. Solitude is healthy and a discipline that should be adopted in moderation. However, constant solitude leads to myopic thinking and a siloed existence. Existing is not living. If you risk being known, you'll become more comfortable no matter who you're with — even when you're just by yourself.

THINK

How have I isolated myself?

MEDITATE

Today I will risk being known. I will be friendly with the world and with myself. Today I will refuse to let the lonely birds roost in my heart for too long. I will reach out and be open to whoever comes my way. Today I will move towards friendship and community.

LIVE

When loneliness invades my heart, I will be grateful for the relationships I do have.

regret

/rəˈgret/

Every human being misses the mark, but if you hope
to live life to the fullest, you need to own the positive
and negative choices you make.

Day Twelve — Regret

READ

Regret is like a shadow. The only way to lose it is to look towards the light — what is good, true and beautiful in your life. Neurologically, focusing on regret causes your brain to shut down its ability to recognise and experience positive rewards. Regret also sends the 'fight or flight' part of your brain (amygdala) into overdrive scanning your immediate environment for any potential threat. Regret kills pleasure and erodes confidence. Regret literally means, 'to look back with sorrow'. This type of living is backwards. Constantly looking back at past failures, mistakes and missed opportunities can cripple your confidence. Replaying 'what-ifs' and 'woulda-coulda-shouldas' robs you of the ability to be present. The best way forward is to let go of what you cannot change or control. Grieve the loss and failure, then focus on what good is happening now and what good lies ahead.

THINK

What past regret do I need to let go of?

MEDITATE

Today I will let go of my past wounds — my failures and mistakes. I will not let the past determine my future. Today I will embrace who I am becoming. I will not let failure define me. Today I will use the good and the bad of my story to create a better future.

LIVE

When past regret consumes my thoughts or grips my heart, I will search for the good, true and beautiful in my life.

overthinking

/ˌōvərˈTHiNGk/

Being successful in life is about mindset. It's a choice about truly believing in your innate strengths, talents and abilities. When you change your thinking, you change your life.

Day Thirteen — Overthinking

READ

Overthinking leads to under-living. When you question everything you almost always fail to answer anything. If you're an analytical soul, learning how to shut your mind off long enough to take a risk seems like an impossibility. Nothing is impossible, building confidence takes time. Critical thinking is a blessing and a curse. Over time you can break the sick cycle of being too critical on yourself. Confidence is built by taking calculated risks. However, the danger is you calculating for too long. Eventually you have to jump. Confidence is a byproduct of taking risks.

THINK

How do I psych myself out from taking risks?

MEDITATE

Today I will stop thinking so much and start living. I will choose to trust my intuition more, and learn from my failures. Today I will press pause when my mind begins to spin out of control. I am not my overactive imagination, and I will not allow my worst fears to rule me.

LIVE

When my mind kicks into overdrive, I will slow down, breathe, and take one small step towards life.

chaos

/ˈkāˌäs/

You are part of the busiest, most informed, overworked, overstimulated and overcommitted society in the history of the world. Mindful living is the only remedy for a busy soul.

Day Fourteen — Chaos

READ
Consciously causing chaos in your life is a natural response to boredom. Without a significant challenge you go in search of stimulation. Why? To feel alive — human. Without progress you slowly begin to die. Too much chaos and you go into survival mode, too little and you begin to atrophy. When everything is in flux you have no choice but to sort through the clutter and find a reliable way through. Your brain is a conscious, dynamic and complex organ that processes information on multiple levels. It is self-organising the chaos of your life, into useful and sometimes life- changing perceptions and input. Your brain operates on the edge of chaos most of the time, quietly whirring in the background. Waiting for an interesting challenge where your knowledge, skills and experience can be tested. The result — confidence.

THINK
How has chaos been a playground of personal growth for me?

MEDITATE
Today I will stop thinking about chaos as a threat and see it for what it really is — an opportunity to find out what I'm made of. I won't shrink back from it. Today I will consciously explore and test myself against whatever life throws my way. I will trust in the midst of the storm.

LIVE
I will befriend chaos when it comes my way.

laziness

/ˈlāzēnəs/

Do not imitate.
You may have mimicked others in the past,
but you are only limiting yourself.
Find your own way.

Day Fifteen — Laziness

READ
Shortcuts are tangible excuses. If you're lazy you'll rarely achieve true confidence — because you'll never fully know what you're capable of. Where your strengths lie. Or, how smart you are. At its core laziness is an expression of arrogance. It's self-preservation masked behind convenience. Building confidence requires discipline and ownership. If you're lazy, you simply cannot stomach this type of personal responsibility. You would rather minimise the challenges and difficulty in life, than do the hard work and heavy lifting that real strength demands. The result is a life filled with regret and missed opportunities. If you want to develop self-belief, take action, be proactive.

THINK
What shortcuts am I continuously taking?

MEDITATE
Today I will not cut corners or rush the process. I will consciously count the cost of what I'm facing. Today I will refuse to make excuses. I will be a person of my word and see things all the way through. Today I choose to work.

LIVE
I will not take shortcuts.

faith

/fāTH/

Start small. Focus on small daily wins. Daily rituals. Adopt habits that will lead you to realising your dream.

Day Sixteen — Faith

READ

Faith is the spiritual word for trust. Do you trust yourself? Confidence literally means, 'to trust within'. Self-belief cannot be developed without consistent self-reflection and brutal honesty. Relationships cannot survive without trust. Especially, your relationship with yourself. Confidence is not something that can be faked — that's arrogance. You are who you are. So get to know who you are. Your strengths and your weaknesses. Your likes and your dislikes. Your convictions and your allowances. The greatest journey you can take is a pilgrimage into your own soul. Get curious about you. Figure out who you are and what you believe. And, you'll be believable. Trustworthy. True. Uniquely you.

THINK

Do I trust myself enough to be me?

MEDITATE

Today I will strive for integrity — being the same inside and out. I will not fake confidence or think too little of myself. Today I will be okay being me and knowing what that means. I will be honest with myself and others.

LIVE

I won't be a copy, I'll be an original.

help

/help/

You have to come out of hiding. You have to put down the masks of insecurity. You have to invite people to journey with you. You have to be known.

Day Seventeen — Help

READ

Asking for help is not a sign of weakness. It's a sign of strength. Confident people aren't afraid to admit what they don't know and cannot do. Help is an old English word that means, 'to serve someone food'. At the end of the day isn't that what you really want? To help others find what they genuinely need. And, when you're in need, for people to notice and give a damn. Truly confident people are not obsessed with themselves, nor do they ignore the needs of others. If you want to get over yourself, find someone to help. Better yet, let someone help you.

THINK

Do I allow others to help me?

MEDITATE

Today I will ask for help. I won't see myself as a burden. Today I will be open and willing to help and be helped. When I see a need, in myself or others, I will respectfully speak up and reach out.

LIVE

Today I won't be ruled by false pride, I'll accept assistance however it materialises in my life.

progress

/'prägres/

You already have all you need to live an abundant and remarkable life. Get out of your own way. Let go of the past. Step into your future. Start crafting a life around what really matters to you. Do the necessary things. Get to work.

Day Eighteen — Progress

READ
You are your own worst enemy. You are also the answer to your own prayers. By now you've woken up to the fact if nothing changes, nothing changes. If you truly want to be confident, you will not let fear, or anything else stop you from doing the next right thing. There's a simple principle at work in life: adapt or die. The goal is not perfection, it's progress. An inch, a step, even the smallest movement in the right direction is a start. Just start. Start small. Start now. Stay consistent. Don't give up. View failure as feedback and be grateful every time you have to pick yourself up. Your brain is malleable — remember, it's called neuroplasticity. You can rewire your negative thinking. You can change. You really can. Just start.

THINK
Where am I seeing progress?

MEDITATE
Today I will start. I will take action and stop making excuses. Today I will focus on one small goal and execute it. When I fall down, I will reflect and try a different approach. I'll let failure refine me.

LIVE
Failure is feedback.

perfection

/pər'fekSH(ə)n/

Acknowledge what you're not
and embrace all that you are.
What you lack
highlights what you have to offer.

Day Nineteen — Perfection

READ

Perfection comes from the Latin, 'to complete'. The hard truth is you never arrive. Confidence is fickle. Your mind can trick you. Your old fears can rise up. Your goal is to keep moving. To keep learning. To keep growing. That's where life becomes your teacher. Wisdom is the result of learning what not to do. You are work in progress. Stay on the path towards cultivating self-belief. Keep getting stronger.

Over time you'll be more and more comfortable in your own skin. And, the cancerous voices of self-criticism and self-rejection will fade. Give up on perfection. Instead, seek to be at peace. Stop damning yourself to hell. You're on your own unique path to wholeness.

THINK

How is self-criticism killing my confidence?

MEDITATE

Today I will let go of perfection. I will embrace the impossibility of being without flaws. Today I will build confidence by being grateful for who I am instead of what I'm not. I will live at peace with myself.

LIVE

Perfection is an illusion, humble confidence is not.

must

/məst/

Do not shrink back from challenges. Do not give in to fear. Do not let failure, heartaches, a lack of resources, or the absence of support determine your success.

Day Twenty — Must

READ

What's the one thing that you 'must' do today? Confidence comes from clarity. Being laser focused on achieving your priorities is key in building self-belief. Asking yourself if you have what it takes to successfully complete what you said 'yes' to.

Overcoming fear and trepidation no matter how big or small the challenge. Pacing yourself and slowly gaining momentum. These are all crucial elements in confidently tackling your challenges. 'Must' comes from the Germanic word müssen, it means, 'that which has to be done, seen, or experienced'. Having clarity about what you 'must' do today is one of the greatest gifts you can give yourself.

You have to know what you're aiming at if you hope to hit the target.

THINK

What must I do today?

MEDITATE

Today I will focus on a short list of my priorities. When fear and uncertainty pop up, I'll return to what I must do. Today I will focus. I won't let distractions or detours stop me. Today I will be confident about facing my goals.

LIVE

I will focus on what's essential.

self-care

/self ker/

Say no. No to distractions. No to energy stealers. No to old patterns of thinking. No to anyone and anything which isn't going to help you achieve what you need to achieve today.

Day TwentyOne — Self-Care

READ
Taking care of yourself is not a selfish act. When you are healthy you have something tangible to offer others. When you are constantly running on empty, beat up and burnt out — what can you possibly hope to give? You running around from one emergency to the next helps no one. Especially you. The goal is to be in flow with the world around you. Not constantly fighting a tide of negativity, conflict and toxic choices. Slowing down eventually speeds you up. Taking care of yourself may feel selfish at first, but you'll have so much more to give if you put your own oxygen mask on first. Think about it. How confident can you be in your abilities when you're not your best self? Internal strength requires intentional nourishment.

THINK
What is my biggest personal need today?

MEDITATE
Today I will stop trying to be everything for everyone. I will take care of myself physically, mentally, emotionally and spiritually. Today I will choose me. I will intentionally slow down and take stock of how I am doing.

LIVE
I will take care of myself today.

risk

/risk/

Do not test the waters with trepidation.
Do not hesitate when opportunity presents itself.
Do not shrink back from challenges.

Day TwentyTwo — Risk

READ
Roughly 70 percent of the population is risk averse. The other 30 percent view risk-taking as a way of life. You either love or hate this little four letter word. 'Risk' comes from the French word for 'danger'. How you define risk determines the volatility and direction of your life. Confident people are okay taking healthy risks. If that's not you, some past failure has probably marked you in some profound way. Every relationship requires some sort of risk. When you open yourself up to another human being you risk rejection. When you leave a career you've known all your life you risk having to start all over again. Confident people count the cost. Confident people ask for feedback from family and friends. Confident people are okay making the jump. Why? Past experience — failures and successes — help them trust they can do it again.

THINK
How do I feel about risk?

MEDITATE
Today I will revisit past risks I've taken and what they taught me. I will not be afraid of setting out in a new direction. Today I will trust myself and my judgement. I won't let past hurt or failure define my future.

LIVE
I will not shrink back from fear of failure. I will risk!

consistency

/kənˈsistənsē/

Keep coming back to the truth of your calling. To the idea that captured your heart. To the work you alone must do. Do not listen to the haters. Do not get distracted by the masses.
Choose to live an uncommon life.

Day TwentyThree — Consistency

READ
Consistency is about showing up every day. When you show up on a regular basis you slowly develop discipline. You find out what you're made of, what you can endure and what you cannot tolerate. You also build a track record of small victories — successes. These small wins create a sense of momentum. If you stay long enough, you gain the knowledge, experience and skills you so desperately need to face future challenges. In short, you build confidence. This requires intentionality on your part. There are no half measures when it comes to staying the course and remaining faithful. You'll be tempted to quit, to throw in the towel. Don't do it. Refuse to settle and compromise. The more you exercise this type of personal perseverance, the stronger you become mentally.

THINK
What should I not quit on today?

MEDITATE
Today I will stay the course and honour my commitments. I will learn from being present, here — now. Today I will be vigilant about refining my skills and using them faithfully in the task at hand. I won't underestimate my ability to push through.

LIVE
I will continue to show up.

openness

/ˈōpənˌnəs/

You alone have the power
to be a victim or become a hero.
You alone have the power
to give yourself over to despair or to choose hope.
You alone get to decide whether
your best days are ahead of you or behind you.

Day TwentyFour — Openness

READ

Your willingness to be proven wrong reveals a lot about your confidence. Ideas and originality are indeed sacred, but what's even more holy is your ability to unlearn and relearn difficult truths. Teachability and continuous learning are hallmarks of humble souls. Learning how to not take conflict and disagreements so personally is a journey worth every step. Trusting yourself — self-belief — requires letting go of the need to control outcomes and others. When you hold everything with an open hand, you'll begin to see all of life as a gift. Highs and lows will come, but you will have an inner strength and resolve that cannot be easily shaken. Confidence requires an open mind and growth mindset.

THINK

Where have I closed myself off from people, ideas, risks, opportunities?

MEDITATE

Today I will be open to being proven wrong. I will remain curious about life and different perspectives. Today I will choose to be teachable. I will not shut people out or stop listening simply because I feel threatened. Today I will allow others in.

LIVE

I will let go of my need to be in total control.

honesty

/ˈänəstē/

Words are merely surface-level indicators of deeply held beliefs. When you are squeezed, tested and pushed, the words that come into your mind and flow out of your mouth reveal where you are and who you really are.

Day TwentyFive — Honesty

READ

'Honesty' comes from the 13th century French root of the word 'honour' which means, 'glory'. There is something glorious about a soul that is truthful. When you're deeply honest — inside and out — you can be trusted. People will have confidence in you and your ability. And, so will you. If you aren't who you say you are, you cannot be trusted. Trust is what every relationship is built on. Being honest with another human being is a scary thing, but it's the only way to become whole — confident.

THINK

What secrets or lies are keeping me from being me?

MEDITATE

Today I will be honest. I won't sugarcoat the truth, especially with myself. Today I will not live secretly and I will not be ashamed of my past. Instead, I will choose to be honest about the good and bad in me. I will be who I say I am — inside and out.

LIVE

I will be the real me today, no more, no less.

willingness

/'wiliNGnəs/

You have to be willing to reinvent yourself. You have to be willing to challenge your old ways of thinking. You have to be willing to push beyond the status quo.

Day TwentySix — Willingness

READ
It's your willingness to adapt, change and grow that determines how confident you will be in the face of uncertainty. True willingness requires movement and action. You can't just desire change. You must be willing to burn the boats and take a step in a new direction. This is where your confidence will be tested. It is unsettling—literally. You must strike out from your little bird's nest on the ground in order to take flight. Complacency is the enemy of progress. It's a pleasurable and comfortable trap. You feel good for the moment, but if you're honest you have stopped willingly taking risks. That is the curse of trying to protect what you have, you can never live a generous life. You must be willing to give up what you have today to create a better future tomorrow. You're not done yet.

THINK
What is holding me back from acting on my desire to grow and change?

MEDITATE
Today I will be more than willing. Today I will act. Confidently and consciously. I won't settle for table scraps and limited success. I will not settle for mediocracy. Today I will stop focusing on what I might lose, and instead explore what I might gain.

LIVE
I will be willing to lose in order to win.

kindness

/ˈkīn(d)nəs/

Let your life be good news. Be known by your compassion and your conviction. When you become more, you have more to give back to others.

Day TwentySeven — Kindness

READ
It doesn't take much to be kind, but the impact it has on you and others can be profound. Being kind to yourself and others takes intentionality and effort. And being kind to yourself takes real guts.

Self-Kindness, learning how to celebrate your successes and forgive your failures, is key to building confidence. The starting place is — and always will be — gratitude. Feeling inadequate? Make a list of your top three strengths. Think you are a massive fraud? You are just like everyone else. Human. Flawed. The good news is you belong.

Kindness comes from the German word for 'family'. So be kind to yourself and others. Your brothers and sisters of the world need you…to be you. You are vital and one of a kind.

THINK
Where am I being unkind to myself?

MEDITATE
Today I will be kind to myself and others. I will choose to believe that I belong. Today I will be grateful for who I am and who I am becoming. When feelings of inadequacy and being 'found out' come, I will remember to be kind.

LIVE
I will be one of a kind — me.

humility

/(h)yōˑoˈmilədē/

Ask questions. Listen. Acknowledge your failures.
Learn from others. Wisdom comes from falling down
and then getting back up.

Day TwentyEight — Humility

READ

Humility is having an accurate view of yourself. The root of Humility is 'humus' the Latin word for 'earth or dirt'. To be humble is to have both feet on the ground.

Confident people don't think too highly — arrogance — or too lowly — self-pity — of themselves. When you're humble it's almost impossible to offend you. You are confident about who you are and clear about what you're not. If you struggle with humility chances are you've avoided challenges, because true humility comes through humiliations — being knocked down and knocked back. There's a reason pride knocks you over eventually. You are meant to keep your feet on the ground.

THINK

Where is arrogance crippling me?

MEDITATE

Today I will be okay just being me. I won't boast or brag or puff up with false confidence. I will take a deep breath and get comfortable in my own skin. Today I won't be more or less than. Today I will simply be ... me.

LIVE

I will keep both feet on the ground.

generosity

/jenəˈräsədē/

As you go throughout your day, be grateful. Cultivate an attitude of thankfulness. Gratitude frees you from the grip of self. Gratitude moves you to take continued and sustained action towards generosity.

Day TwentyNine — Generosity

READ

Generosity is a way of life for confident people. You know you're okay on the inside when you give to others without expecting anything in return. If living a generous life seems foreign and strange to you, it's quite possible that you are still insecure at your core. Try giving something you need away. That small act of defiance against your ego will chip away at your fear of not having or being enough. You'll begin to trust yourself more. And, you'll be trusted with more. It is quite easy to have a false sense of security when you have a lot. Your external resources don't make you who you are. It's your inner resources — confidence and character — that make you, you. Generous is a 15th century French word meaning, 'of noble birth'. Living a generous life will empower you to give others what they need to live a better, more full life. That is real nobility. That is what confidence does. It's contagious.

THINK

Who can I really help today?

MEDITATE

Today I will take a hard look at whether I own my stuff, or if it owns me. I will strive to see the needs of others around me and not just my own. Today I will embrace generosity as a way of life. I will give more than I take.

LIVE

I will be prepared to give from the inside out.

confidence

/ˈkänfədəns/

Stop playing small. Let go of your limiting beliefs.
Cultivate a life of growth and share what you learn
with others.

Day Thirty — Confidence

READ

Confidence is a byproduct of taking risks. If you lack confidence you probably are playing it safe. You may have even settled. This type of small-minded living feels secure, but it will slowly lull your soul to sleep. Before too long you'll be numb inside. That's a sure sign apathy has gripped your heart. Wake up before atrophy sets in. The greatest gift you can give yourself — and the world — is to take a risk that makes you feel alive again. Don't lose heart, everyone can change. Even you. You've been hiding out for far too long. What are you really afraid of? Losing something? You're absolutely going to lose something. Maybe even everything. If you try to live, to adventure — not just exist — you're guaranteed to get beat up, broken, disappointed and disillusioned. But, guess what? You'll also be stronger, more confident and wiser as a result. So which kind of life are you going to choose?

THINK

What has playing it safe cost me?

MEDITATE

Today I will leave the known for the unknown. I will let go of safety and security and white-knuckle living. Today I will trust myself. I will back myself no matter how fearful or insecure I feel. Today I will live. I won't just exist.

LIVE

I will believe in me.

courage

/ˈkərij/

Rediscover your imagination. Rekindle your childlike wonder. Reignite your passion for learning. Shine bright so others can see the way forward too.

Day ThirtyOne — Courage

READ

Courageous people are just scared souls who were compelled to act. Most of the time, with little or no fanfare. No one around to cheer them on, or bear witness.

Courageous because the world needed them to be. Courage is the tangible expression of people who believe in themselves — a genuinely confident human being. This kind of living is infectious. When you back yourself and believe you have what it takes, you give others permission to do the same. Humble and self- assured, your life will take on a kind of unstoppable quality. Quietly going about the business of living. Serving from a place of abundance at your core. No longer needing the approval or permission of others. You. Alive. Free. And, focused. Clear about who you are and what you have to offer this spinning ball of dirt. Unafraid and unashamed to be you no matter who you're with or what's required of you. That life is possible, if you want it to be.

THINK

Where am I compelled to act?

MEDITATE

Today I will pay attention to my heart. I will live from the core of who I am. Unafraid and unashamed to be me and do what needs to be done. I won't let fear or failure be an excuse to stop living. Today I will confidently serve, especially when no one is looking.

LIVE

I will trust my intuition and follow my heart.

DEFINITIONS

All definitions were sourced from these two sources:

Online Etymology Dictionary. 2001 — 2017 Douglas Harper, accessed 01 January 2017 <https://www.etymonline.com/>

Dictionary.com. 1995 — 2017 Dictionary.com, LLC, accessed 01 January 2017 <http://www.dictionary.com/>

Worry

Old English wyrgan "to strangle," of West Germanic origin, and in Middle English "to seize by the throat and tear."

Insecurity

1640s, "state of being unsafe," also "lack of assurance or confidence, apprehension," from Medieval Latin *insecuritas*, from insecurus.

Fear

Middle English fere, from Old English fær "calamity, sudden danger, peril, sudden attack."

Hopelessness

1560s, "offering no grounds for hope," from hope (n.) + -less. From 1580s as "having no expectation of success."

Apathy

c. 1600, "freedom from suffering, passionless existence," from French apathie (16c.)

Avoidance

late 14c., "action of emptying," from avoid + -ance. Sense of "action of dodging or shunning" is recorded from early 15c.

Comfort

c. 1200, "feeling of relief" (as still in to take comfort in something); also "source of alleviation or relief;" from Old French confort.

People-Pleasing

early 14c., "to be agreeable," from Old French plaisir "to please, give pleasure to, satisfy."

Conflict

early 15c., "armed encounter, battle," from Old French conflit and directly from Latin conflictus.

Boredom

"practice of being a bore" (1840, a sense properly belonging to boreism, 1833).

Isolation

"to set or place apart, to detach so as to make alone," by 1786.

Regret

"pain or distress in the mind at something done or left undone," 1530s.

Overthinking

Old English þencan "imagine, conceive in the mind; consider, meditate, remember; intend, wish, desire."

Chaos

late 14c., "gaping void; empty, immeasurable space," from Old French chaos (14c.)

Laziness

1540s, laysy, of persons, "averse to labor, action, or effort," a word of unknown origin.

Faith

from Anglo-French and Old French feid, foi "faith, belief, trust, confidence; pledge" (11c.)

Help

Old English help (m.), helpe (f.) "assistance, succor."

Progress

late 14c., "a going on, action of walking forward," from Old French progres.

Perfection

early 15c. alteration of Middle English parfit (c. 1300), from Old French parfit "finished, completed, ready" (11c.)

Must

Old English moste, past tense of motan "have to, be able to," from Proto-Germanic *mot- "ability, leisure (to do something)."

Self-Care

Old English caru, cearu "sorrow, anxiety, grief," also "burdens of mind; serious mental attention."

Risk

1660s, risque, from French risque (16c.), from Italian risco, riscio (modern rischio), from riscare "run into danger."

Consistency

1590s, "firmness of matter," from Medieval Latin consistentia or directly from Latin consistentem.

Openness

Old English open "not closed down, raised up."

Honesty

early 14c., "splendor, honor; elegance," later "honorable position; propriety of behavior, good manners; virginity, chastity" (late 14c.)

Willingness

Old English will, willa "mind, determination, purpose; desire, wish, request; joy, delight," from Proto- Germanic *wiljon.

Kindness

c. 1300, "courtesy, noble deeds."

Humility

early 14c., "quality of being humble," from Old French umelite "humility, modesty, sweetness."

Generosity

early 15c., "nobility, goodness of race," from Latin generositatem (nominative generositas).

Confidence

early 15c., from Middle French confidence or directly from Latin confidentia, from confidentem (nominative confidens) "firmly trusting, bold," present participle of confidere "to have full trust or reliance."

Courage

c. 1300, from Old French corage (12c., Modern French courage) "heart, innermost feelings; temper."

SOURCES

Lak A, Costa G, Romberg E, Koulakov A, Mainen Z, Kepecs A. 'Orbitofrontal Cortex Is Required for Optimal Waiting Based on Decision Confidence'. *Neuron*, vo. 84 issue 1, accessed 01 May 2017, <http://www.cell.com/neuron/fulltext/S0896-6273(14)00740-5>

Gardner B, Lally P, Wardle J. 'Making health habitual: the psychology of 'habit-formation' and general practice'. *British Journal of General Practice*, vo. 62(605), accessed 01 May 2017, <https://www.ncbi.nlm.nih.gov/pmc/articles/PMC3505409/>

Doidge N. (2007) *The Brain That Changes Itself: Stories of Personal Triumph from the Frontiers of Brain Science.* New York, New York: Penguin Books Ltd.

Sanders JI, Hangya B, Kepecs A. 'Signatures of a Statistical Computation in the Human Sense of Confidence'. *Neuron*, vo. 90 issue 3, accessed 01 May 2017, <http://www.cell.com/neuron/fulltext/S0896-6273(16)30016-2>

Shermer M. 'Patternicity: Finding Meaningful Patterns in Meaningless Noise'. *Scientific American*, published 01 December 2008 and accessed 01 May 2017, <https://www.scientificamerican.com/article/patternicity-finding-meaningful-patterns/>

ABOUT THE AUTHOR

Steve Knox is an expert on Leadership and Team Culture. Through assessment, coaching and consulting, Steve has impacted over 300+ organisations and 250,000+ people over the past 15 years. They include Fortune 500 companies, small businesses and not-for-profit organisations throughout the world.

As a facilitator, Steve has the rare ability to engage and equip an audience with powerful insights and practical tools for creating lasting change and providing individuals with a better way to live and work.

He holds an MA in Entrepreneurial Leadership and is the author of two books, including *The Asymmetrical Leader: Embrace Your Weaknesses, Unleash Your Strengths.*

In 2017, Steve co-founded **imprint** — the world's simplest personality assessment tool. To date, 10,000+ individuals have been assessed, and 50,000+ have experienced **imprint** online. Discover how you're wired to lead at imprinttest.com.

Have a question?

Continue the conversation with Steve here:

steve@steveknox.us

@knox_orbiting

www.steveknox.us

Printed in Australia
AUOW01n0934130218
294635AU00004B/4

9 780648 130000